CONCUSSIONS
IN SPORTS

BY MARYANN HUDSON

Published by ABDO Publishing Company, PO Box 398166, Minneapolis, MN 55439. Copyright © 2014 by Abdo Consulting Group, Inc. International copyrights reserved in all countries. No part of this book may be reproduced in any form without written permission from the publisher. SportsZone™ is a trademark and logo of ABDO Publishing Company.

Printed in the United States of America,
North Mankato, Minnesota
102013
012014

 THIS BOOK CONTAINS AT LEAST 10% RECYCLED MATERIALS.

Editor: Chrös McDougall
Series Designer: Craig Hinton

Photo credits: Eric Bellamy, The Daily Tribune/AP Images, cover, 1; Tony Quinn/Icon SMI, 5, 13; Paul Kitagaki Jr., The Sacramento Bee/AP Images, 7; Ed Rieker/AP Images for National Football League, 10; Aspen Photo/Shutterstock Images, 15, 27; Shutterstock Images, 18; David Duprey/AP Images, 22; Lyle E. Doberstein/Shutterstock Images, 25; Kathy Willens/AP Images, 30; Will Schneekloth/Icon SMI, 32; Craig Lassig/AP Images for Dick's Sporting Goods, 34; Gretchen Ertl/AP Images, 37; Haessly Photography/Shutterstock Images, 39; Dave Martin/AP Images, 42; Zumapress/Icon SMI, 44; iStockphoto, 46; Amy Sancetta/AP Images, 49; Ben Margot/AP Images, 50; Paul Chiasson, The Canadian Press/AP Images, 53; Jim Stroup, Virginia Tech via Richmond Times-Dispatch/AP Images, 56; Gerald Herbert/AP Images, 59

Library of Congress Control Number: 2013946575

Cataloging-in-Publication Data

Hudson, Maryann.
 Concussions in sports / Maryann Hudson.
  p. cm. -- (Issues in sports)
Includes bibliographical references and index.
ISBN 978-1-62403-120-5
1. Sports injuries--Juvenile literature. 2. Brain--Concussion--Juvenile literature. I. Title.
617.4--dc23

2013946575

Content Consultants:
Chris Zacko MD, MS, Co-Director of Neurotrauma and Neurocritical Care
Head of Penn State Neurologic Sports Injury Program, Assistant Professor of Neurosurgery
Penn State Milton S. Hershey Medical Center

Jonathon Cooke, MD, Neurosurgery Resident
Penn State Milton S. Hershey Medical Center

TABLE OF CONTENTS

THE GAME CHANGER

Abby Wambach hardly had time to react. Her teammate kicked the soccer ball hard to clear it away from the goal. Wambach was positioned a few yards away. And before Wambach knew it, the ball knocked her straight in the head. Suddenly the star player collapsed to the ground. She clutched her head and rolled into the fetal position.

The referee came to Wambach's side and began asking her questions. Wambach, still on the ground, said she was fine. After all, it was a close game. Her Western New York Flash were tied 1–1 with the Washington Spirit in their National Women's Soccer League (NWSL) game. Only a

minute remained in the game. So Wambach wanted to stay in. The referee took her word. She motioned to the trainer not to come on the field. Teammates patted Wambach and walked away.

Wambach struggled to get up. It took her 31 seconds. She rolled to her knees, stood slowly, and took a few off-balance steps. Then she stayed in the game.

The referee resumed play. Wambach continued to press forward in search of a goal. She had an opportunity when her team was awarded a late corner kick. Wambach tried to head the cross into the goal. It didn't work. Then the final whistle blew, and Wambach fell to her knees.

Spirit goalie Ashlyn Harris said Wambach looked dazed. Harris motioned for help and asked Wambach if she was okay. Wambach only mumbled. A trainer rushed to Wambach and helped her off the field.

"She is such a tough competitor," said Harris, who is Wambach's teammate on the US national team. "She is just relentless and not going to take herself out."

That tough attitude might have been praised in the past. But this game was on April 20, 2013. Awareness of brain injuries in sports was at an all-time high. The Centers for Disease Control and Prevention (CDC) is a leader in concussion research. From 2001 to 2009, the CDC estimated a 62 percent increase in emergency room visits for sports and recreation-related brain injuries. Most of the injuries were concussions. By 2009, there were approximately 250,000 visits each year. The highest rates were

among males from 10 to 19 years old. In general, though, experts say that the number for sports-related concussions is much higher than these figures would indicate. Many concussions go unreported or are untreated.

Wambach took a big risk by staying in that game. The league took a big risk by letting her stay in. And with people caring more than ever about the seriousness of concussions in athletes, the injury did not go unnoticed.

WHAT IS A CONCUSSION?

A concussion changes the way the brain normally works. A concussion happens when the brain is shaken inside the skull and causes a change in alertness. This feeling can range from being a little off to blacking out. Even "seeing stars" qualifies as a sign of concussion.

The word concussion comes from the Latin word *concutere*. It means "to shake violently." This shaking of the brain can be caused by a bump, blow, or jolt to the head. It can also come from a blow to the body that causes the brain to shake or spin rapidly.

Brain injuries can be very dangerous. The brain is the body's command center. Concussions affect the brain's ability to communicate with the rest of the body. When this happens, patients might experience painful headaches, memory problems, trouble with learning, fatigue, and depression.

Approximately 90 percent of concussions are resolved quickly. Most are resolved within 7 to 10 days. In some cases, however, symptoms can stay for a long time or even forever. Plus, symptoms can worsen if a person suffers another jolt before making a full recovery. In the most serious cases a second jolt can even be fatal. It is called second-impact syndrome.

Concussions fall under the medical category of traumatic brain injury (TBI). A TBI occurs when normal brain function is disrupted by a bump or a jolt. However, TBIs can vary in severity. A concussion is called a mild traumatic brain injury (MTBI). That is because it is not usually life-threatening.

"[An MTBI is] only mild compared to the train wreck of severe TBI that can leave you in the hospital for years," Dr. Douglas Smith wrote in the book *The Concussion Crisis*. "But for people with concussions that just want to get back to being themselves, it's not mild at all."

SCIENTISTS, THE NFL, AND JOHN MADDEN

Scientists, researchers, and organizations have led the charge with warnings about the danger of concussions. Meanwhile, statistics show that concussions in sports are increasing. Between 1997 and 2007, the number of 8- to 13-year-olds going to the emergency room with sports-related concussions doubled. The number of visits tripled among 14- to 19-year-olds. Researchers aren't certain if the increase is due to more concussions or more awareness of the issue.

Either way, what is certain is that more people are paying attention. Part of that is due to high-profile concussions. The National Football League (NFL) is the most popular sports league in the United States. For years the league denied any connection between football and brain injuries. However, scientists studied the brains of deceased former players and discovered serious brain damage. In 2009, the NFL acknowledged a connection between football and symptoms associated with

THE NUMBERS

The CDC studied sports-related concussions for people between the ages of 10 and 19. From 2001 to 2009, males suffered more sports-related concussions in football and bicycling than any other sports. After that, basketball, baseball, and soccer saw the most concussions. Females of the same age suffered more concussions from soccer, basketball, and bicycling. Overall, bicycling is the leading cause of sports-related head injuries in children under 14. The number of concussions in bicycling is nearly double that of football. And in children younger than nine, concussions from bicycling and playground sports are most common.

brain injuries. It soon issued a warning to players that read: "Concussions and conditions resulting from repeated brain injury can change your life and your family's life forever."

This was one of the most important turning points in concussion awareness. The NFL is now a leader in concussion education and research. The league is also changing rules of the game to make it safer.

Since 2010, dozens of youth clinics specializing in concussions have opened in the United States. Nearly every state has passed laws governing how to handle a player on the sideline after a hard blow to the head. And some experts have gone so far as to suggest that youths 14 years old or younger should not play collision sports. Collision sports are those where colliding is part of the play, such as football and hockey. Contact sports are sports where accidental or unintentional contact is made, such as basketball and soccer.

Many sports leagues, recreation leagues, and schools now have required concussion guidelines. Manufacturers are seeking ways to make equipment more protective. Awareness has even spread to video games. The popular *Madden NFL* games now show players suffering concussions and sitting out the rest of the game.

"It starts with young kids—they start in video games," said John Madden, the former NFL commentator and Pro Football Hall of Fame coach for whom the game is named. "I think the osmosis is if you get a concussion that's a serious thing and you shouldn't play. We want that message to be strong."

SECOND-IMPACT SYNDROME

One concussion can be dangerous. A second concussion before the first one has healed is even more dangerous. This is called second-impact syndrome. The result can be permanent brain damage or death. It does not have to be a hard hit. It can even be a minor hit. The second hit leads to massive brain swelling almost immediately. Brain death can happen in as little as three minutes. Many state laws and guidelines now account for second-impact syndrome. Many states now require athletes to be immediately checked out after a blow to the body or the head. States also try to limit athletes returning to play after a concussion.

TIME FOR PLAYERS TO STEP UP

There have been many advances in research and awareness. But studies indicate that players still need to take concussions more seriously. A 2013 study asked high school football players about concussions. Most of them said they understood the seriousness of playing with a concussion. But only half of the players said they would sometimes or always tell their coach if they had symptoms. And, if a game was important, some players said they would play regardless of a concussion.

All of which brings this back to Wambach. Stefan Fatsis is a reporter for *Slate.com*. He was at the April 20, 2013, game with his 10-year-old daughter when Wambach was hit. He called the event frightening. Fatsis noted that many young soccer players idolize Wambach. They want to be just like her. He believes Wambach sent the wrong message by staying in the game.

"For every step forward in recognizing and treating brain injuries in sports, the jock culture takes a step backward," he wrote.

Wambach sat out the next two games after her hit. Both the NWSL and Wambach insisted that she was fine. They said she was sitting out as a precaution. Wambach finally returned to play 11 days later. At that point the league finally admitted it had been wrong.

In a statement, the league said that Wambach had shown signs of a concussion on the field. The league said the referee should have let the trainer on the field check Wambach's condition before play resumed. The league also reported that the medical staff did examine Wambach

Slate.com writer Stefan Fatsis highlighted soccer ▲ star Abby Wambach in the hope that people could learn from her concussion.

after the game and found signs of a concussion. Those symptoms were confirmed the next day. Wambach then followed the league guidelines and was eventually cleared to play.

Wambach regained her normal brain function. But the incident was one of many that showed the attitudes toward concussion awareness, prevention, and treatment are changing in today's sports culture.

CHAPTER 2

DO NOT DISTURB

T he quarterback took the snap and the play began to develop. The right side of the field opened up. That movement created space for the running back, and he charged through it. It quickly became a one-on-one situation. Freshman linebacker Mark Gould went in to make the tackle for Maranatha High School in Pasadena, California.

The running back, though, was much bigger than Mark. So Mark slid down to grab hold of the running back's legs to trip him. But the running back's thigh came up and under Mark's facemask. Mark's head was knocked back in a very violent way.

"As the play finished, I got up and also got congrats from my fellow teammates for the tackle," Mark said. "The form was correct, and the hit was hard. I was still amped and didn't notice much until about two more plays happened and I started to feel extremely off."

Mark said he felt "a little shaken up." But he said he didn't feel the hit was anything serious.

"[I was mostly] taught with a mentality that you are going to get hit or deliver hits, and it may hurt a bit, but that in the end I would be fine," he said.

But he was not fine. Two plays later he still felt exhausted and extremely sick. He decided he would rather be safe than sorry. Mark told the coach his head was hurting. The school's medical trainer tested Mark on the sidelines for signs of a concussion. Then the trainer called Mark's mom down from the stands.

"Mark showed some signs of a concussion and stayed out of the game, and he seemed to be OK," said Kathy Showerman Gould, Mark's mom. "But at home several hours later he was in excruciating pain in his head. We took him to emergency and they said he did have a concussion and gave him medication for the nausea and pain."

For the next couple of months, this injury that no one could see changed Mark's daily life drastically.

HOW IT HAPPENED

Mark's head snapped back on the play. That caused his brain to spin or shake inside the skull. The brain is soft, like Jell-O, and floats in fluid. It is only loosely anchored. A direct hit or a whiplash-type motion can cause the brain to shake, spin, or do both. And when this happens, the brain slams into the skull, which is rough. But even if the brain doesn't slam into the skull there can be a concussion. The rapid movement alone can cause damage to its soft tissue.

GETTING TECHNICAL: THE HEAD OF IT ALL

The brain has about 50 billion to 100 billion brain cells, or neurons. They are connected by axons. Axons are threadlike fibers that function like a phone cable. They carry information to other cells. But axons are delicate in preadult brains. When the brain is shaken violently, cells and axons are stretched and sheared. Cell communication breaks down. A chemical reaction occurs. The brain is confused. Therefore, the injured person becomes confused as well. The immediate signs of a concussion include confusion, amnesia, dizziness, and disorientation.

////////////////

THE FORCE

The brain moves when it suffers a major jolt. There are two different accelerations, or forces, that determine the direction it moves. A linear acceleration is a straight-line force. It snaps the head violently, such as what happens in a car accident. When hit from the front, the brain hits the back of the skull and then the front of the skull. A side impact results in side-to-side movement of the brain. A rotational acceleration is more damaging. It happens when an off-center jolt causes the brain to rotate or spin within the skull. This might happen when a player is tackled from an angle.

////////////////////

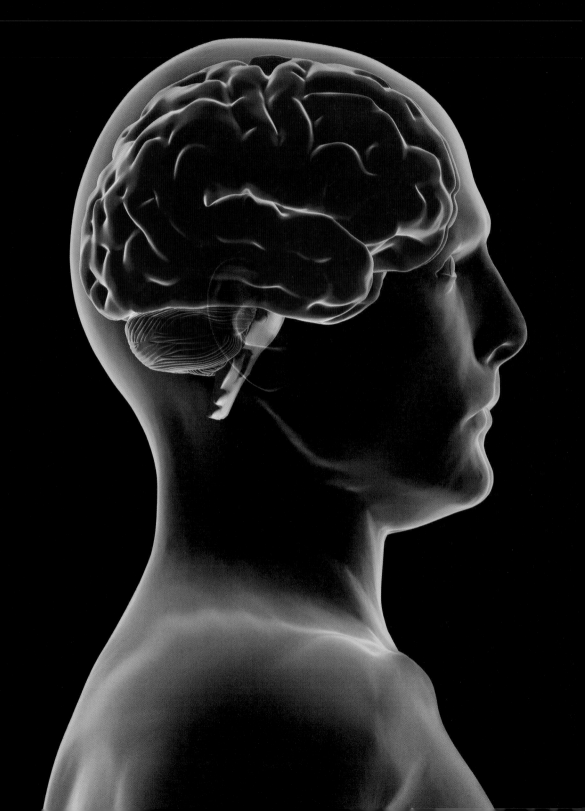

The brain can go into overdrive after a concussion. It summons all its fuel (glucose) to the injury for healing. But there can be a breakdown in the brain's fuel demand, production, and delivery.

In the 24 to 72 hours after a concussion, the brain's energy crisis increases. Experts say this might explain why symptoms, such as painful headaches, do not set in for hours or days after the injury.

THE INVISIBLE INJURY: DIAGNOSING A CONCUSSION

There is no test that allows a doctor to see how much damage has been done to the brain in a concussion. Brain scans can detect internal bleeding, but do not show concussions. Doctors diagnose concussions by observing the symptoms, understanding how the injury occurred, and relying on the athletes to say what they feel.

"What do I see? I see nothing," said Dr. Charles Niesen, Mark Gould's neurologist. "I have to rely on the honesty and compliance of the patient. It's all we have to go on."

Different parts of the brain control different functions. For example, one section controls memory while another controls speech. This means that some functions of the brain might continue to operate normally during a concussion while other functions do not.

During the fast pace of a game, a player might suffer a concussion and not know it. Coaches, teammates, and others are encouraged to help recognize the immediate signs of a possible concussion in a player. Safe Kids Worldwide is an organization founded by the Children's National Medical Center. It put together a concussions guide for youth and high school coaches. The guide lists immediate symptoms for coaches and others to watch for:

- Appears dazed or stunned (such as glossy eyes)
- Is confused about assignment or position
- Forgets an instruction or play
- Is unsure of score or opponent
- Moves clumsily or poor balance
- Answers questions slowly
- Loses consciousness (even briefly)
- Shows mood, behavior, or personality changes
- Can't recall events prior to hit or fall
- Can't recall events after hit or fall

Source: "Concussion Guide for Youth and High School Coaches." Safe Kids Worldwide. Safe Kids Worldwide, 2013. Web. 7 Sept. 2013.

Back It Up

Your football teammate is a little slow getting up after a tough hit, and you think he's probably recovering from the tackle. But as he walks to the huddle, you notice he's off balance. He says he's okay, but you're not so sure. What should you do? Write a paragraph about what you would or would not do, and explain why.

Doctors rarely can determine a concussion's severity right away. Usually they have to wait until the patient recovers. The length and scale of the recovery might help determine the concussion's severity. However, that link is still being investigated.

THE BRAIN HAS ITS OWN CLOCK: TIMETABLE FOR HEALING

Doctors say that 90 percent of concussions heal within 7 to 10 days. There is no official rule, though. The brain operates on its own timetable. Brain tissue does not regenerate. That means cells cannot die off and form new cells. Eventually, the white blood cells get in there and the work begins to repair the damaged brain tissue.

Healing depends on many factors. Some of those include the degree of injury and genetics. Healing can also be slowed or complicated by previous concussions. In addition, psychological conditions can complicate healing. Examples of these include depression and attention deficit hyperactivity disorder (ADHD).

Doctors do not consider a concussion healed until all symptoms are gone. The greatest concern during that time is making sure the brain is fully healed. If not, doctors say the athlete should continue to rest. A second blow to the head while the brain is still injured could cause second-impact syndrome. This can lead to irreparable brain damage or death. And it doesn't take a violent hit on the second blow to cause the damage.

TREATING CONCUSSIONS

To the brain, a concussion is exhausting. Experts say resting immediately after the injury can help recovery. Unfortunately, this means no video games, no computer, and no texting. A little television and reading is sometimes allowed. A concussion can also mean no school for some of the time and no homework, either.

A concussion is easier to understand if it is thought of like a broken leg. A person cannot walk on a broken leg before it is healed. It is the same with the brain. The longer it rests, the better and faster the damage can heal. There is no medication to help the brain to heal. However, doctors may prescribe something to help with some of the symptoms, including nausea and headaches.

Doctors will advise patients as the symptoms lessen. As that happens, the patient can return slowly to daily activities such as work or school. Returning to a sport sometimes takes longer. Doctors and schools usually require all of the symptoms to be gone first. One way to determine that is through exertion tests. They require an athlete to complete an activity such as climbing or running up stairs. If the symptoms return, then the athlete is not yet ready to play.

Sometimes athletes also have to take cognitive performance tests. Before the season they are given a baseline test. This takes information while the brain is functioning normally. The second test can compare the athlete's performance to the first test. If the two tests are similar,

RANKING THE SPORTS

Concussion rates for high school sports can vary according to different studies. But usually the results are similar. Generally, the highest concussion rates for boys are in football, ice hockey, and lacrosse. Girls suffer fewer concussions overall. However, they have higher rates than boys in soccer, basketball, and softball/baseball. The website momsTEAM analyzed two studies that looked at concussion rates among high school athletes. Per 100,000 athletic exposures (an athlete competing for any length of time in an organized game or practice), the rates were:

1. Football: 64 – 76.8
2. Boys' ice hockey: 54
3. Boys' lacrosse: 40 – 46.6
4. Girls' soccer: 33
5. Girls' lacrosse: 31 – 35
6. Girls' field hockey: 22 – 24.9
7. Boys' wrestling: 22 – 23.9
8. Boys' soccer: 19 – 19.2
9. Girls' basketball: 18.6 – 21
10. Boys' basketball: 16 – 21.2

it suggests brain function is back to normal. That helps measure the athlete's readiness to return.

GIVING UP FOOTBALL: MARK MAKES THE CALL

Mark Gould found that returning to school was difficult. He had severe headaches and a difficult time concentrating. Dr. Niesen ordered Mark to have a week of total rest. When Mark's symptoms lessened, he returned to school. However, he sometimes could not last more than half a day because his head would hurt so badly. Niesen said this pain occurs when the brain tissue hasn't healed yet. It gets tired and the nerve endings are not resting enough. Mark suffered post-concussion syndrome (PCS). That is when intense symptoms last a long time.

The whole thing was depressing for Mark. He fell behind in school. But slowly, his symptoms improved. Mark eventually passed exertion tests without his symptoms returning. Niesen then cleared Mark to return to football. The season was nearly over by then, though. Mark played out the season but decided not to play anymore.

In an e-mail, Mark explained his decision:

My decision to not play was not hard for me to say to myself, but attempting to say it to my parents and coaches was a different story. At first I thought my parents would disapprove and feel that I needed to try one more season, but their reaction was quite the opposite. I feel that their reaction was greatly influenced by seeing me go through the mental and physical pain that I suffered from getting the concussion.

Football players may get hit many times each ▲
game, increasing their chances of getting
a concussion.

When I had the concussion, I missed out on school, friends, events, and creating connections within my freshman class. I also suffered from not only the initial symptoms of the concussion, but I also suffered from PCS . . . where I suffered from a series of migraines and head pains that seemed to make me incapable of working at my full level.

When I had to tell my coaches [I was quitting] I was extremely nervous because I already knew that I would be pressured into playing again next year, which in the end they did try, but I stayed strong. I personally feel that the brotherhood part of football is something great and should never be missed out on, but when my health begins to affect my academics then taking a break is the right thing to do.

CHAPTER 3

CHANGING THE CULTURE

Through July 2013, 47 states had passed laws about concussions. The laws dealt with how suspected concussions should be handled for youth, club, and school sports. According to the NFL, those laws usually have three main parts:

1. *Athletes, parents, and coaches must be educated about the dangers of concussions each year.*

2. *If a young athlete is suspected of having a concussion, he/she must be removed from a game or practice and not be permitted to return to play. When in doubt, sit them out.*

3. *A licensed health care professional must clear the young athlete to return to play in the subsequent days or weeks.*

If the laws are followed, they can have a great impact. They can save lives. They can also change a culture in sports. Athletes and coaches will no longer feel pressured to "tough it out." But following these laws is not always easy for coaches and athletes. Brady Pennington coached high school football for 28 years in Texas.

THE LYSTEDT LAW

The concussion laws passed in 47 states through July 2013 originated thanks to Zackery Lystedt. The 13-year-old from Washington suffered a concussion during a 2006 football game. However, he was allowed to return to play too soon. And he suffered another concussion. This resulted in second-impact syndrome. Lystedt was hospitalized for nearly two years. He could not eat on his own and could barely move. But he worked hard to gain at least some of his functions back. Now he works to promote awareness and support for brain injuries. The Lystedt Law was first passed in Washington in 2009. NFL commissioner Roger Goodell helped push for other states to pass a similar law.

"Players don't want to look weak in front of their coach," he said. "In the past, you'd tell a player to get a drink of water and shake it off. They didn't want to disappoint their coach, so they'd go back out there. They didn't want other kids to make fun of them either."

Pennington said the culture change starts with the coach.

"He needs to let that kid know that he's not a sissy," Pennington said. "He's not a baby. He's hurt, and you're going to help take care of him. It can't be a one-time meeting, something you tell them at the beginning of the season. You have to keep assuring them that it's OK to tell the coach.

We want you to come and help us take care of you. But without the coach assuring the players, kids won't say anything. They don't want the coach to think less of them."

Many steps have been taken to help educate people about concussions. Coaches and game officials are required to attend education clinics. Players and parents are required to read and sign concussion information sheets. At the preseason meetings, players are urged to be honest and self-report any signs of a concussion. Parents and teammates are reminded to report any signs they might see. After all, coaches cannot see everything that happens during a game or practice.

On game day, however, legislators and researchers can't do much. The responsibility of making these laws work lies with a core group— the coach, player, trainer, and game officials. Parents watching from the stands are the backup and the follow-up.

WATCHING OUT

The signs can be subtle. A player might get up slowly after a hit or be a little off balance. It can be hard to notice these signs. Many high schools and sports leagues now have medical trainers on the sidelines to help keep watch. However, thousands of youth sporting events have no trainer present. In those cases the responsibility falls on the coach. In the case of soccer, the ultimate authority can be the referee.

Girls' soccer ranks fourth among sports for the rate of concussions. Soccer referees are responsible for stopping the game when a player goes

down from a hit. Referees do not stop the game if there is an obvious goal-scoring opportunity. However, they are required to stop the game immediately after the opportunity to score has passed.

"In soccer, concussion [awareness] is the number one priority," said George Noujaim, director of the National Collegiate Athletic Association (NCAA) National Referee Program and California referee administrator. "When there are no trainers or doctors, the coach has the final say unless a referee sees something. Then the referee has the final word. Bottom line is that the coaches play it down and we overdiagnose, but we [are] on the side of caution. The coach may argue, but the referee will say, 'No, the player is not going to play. That's not going to happen.'"

Referees who override coaches can sometimes get an earful. Players can feel caught in the middle. Players want to please their coach. The players think the best way to please the coach is to keep playing. This is one of the main reasons that players are silent even when feeling signs of a concussion.

BREAKDOWN

ESPN The Magazine surveyed coaches, parents, trainers, and players to see if they were following the concussion guidelines. The results found that players weren't quite doing their part. Players were the least concerned

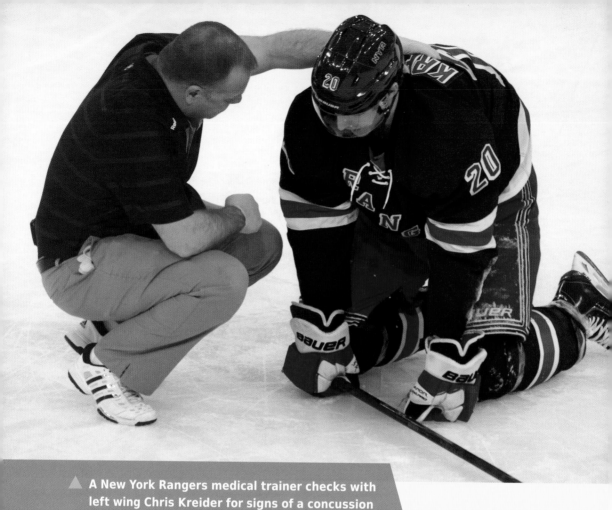

about concussions. Trainers worried the most. Another study surveyed 120 high school football players in the area around Cincinnati, Ohio. More than half of the players said they would continue to play even if they had concussion symptoms.

The reasons players don't self-report vary. Players want to play. They don't want to sit out of a game. They don't want to come out of a game. They don't want to let their teammates down. They don't want to lose

CONCUSSIONS IN SPORTS

their starting spot. They don't want to look weak. They want to show their coach they're tough. They don't want to risk losing a potential scholarship.

IT'S JUST A HEADACHE

A headache is the number one symptom of a concussion. An ESPN survey asked if players should be allowed to return to a game after complaining of a headache. And 55.4 percent of those surveyed said yes. These findings were consistent with what author Brooke de Lench found. She interviewed football players for her documentary *The Smartest Team*. Nearly every football player de Lench interviewed told her they would not self-report concussion symptoms. She believes this silence is encouraged by the culture of collision sports and the young athletes' feelings of being invincible.

THE BUDDY SYSTEM

Teammates can be very important for identifying and reporting concussion signs. That makes it very important for all athletes to understand the risks.

"Those kids are out there, they see things we don't," Pennington said. "We had

SIDELINE TESTING

If a player shows signs of concussion, he or she should be pulled aside and tested. The tests are an overall assessment of the symptoms. They include agility tests as well as mental and cognitive questions. The player is asked questions about the game. These might be as simple as "Who scored last in this match?" or "What venue are we at today?" There are tests to find out if the player is disoriented. The player might be asked what month, day, year, and time it is. Tests can check immediate memory. To do that the player is asked to listen to a list of words and repeat them back. The player might also be asked to repeat a list of numbers and months of the year in reverse order. There are different versions of assessment testing.

▲ Former NFL quarterback Brad Johnson takes the baseline concussion test with a group of young athletes in 2011.

several times last season where a kid would say, 'Hey coach, you have to look at Joe.'"

Parents are another set of eyes. Becky Bates's son Benjamin suffered a concussion when he was in fifth grade. Then Benjamin had another head injury while playing football at age 15. Becky had learned about the risks of concussions. So she decided to pull Benjamin out of the sport for a week for testing. Ultimately he did not have a concussion. He was diagnosed with a migraine headache instead. Becky did not want to take any risks, though.

"I see so many parents and kids try to avoid a diagnosis that might sideline their kids, and there is a lot of ignorance out there still," she told the *Wall Street Journal*.

Pennington agrees. "I've had parents yell, 'He's OK, put him back in,'" Pennington said. "But the bottom line is, I'm going to take care of that kid."

NOT ALL SPORTS ARE CREATED EQUAL

Football and boys seem to get the most attention in sports. But what about when it comes to concussion education and management? Well, yes, football and boys seem to get the most attention.

A study of 235 high schools in Michigan focused on football, boys' and girls' soccer, and boys' ice hockey. It found that there are differences in how much education girls and boys receive.

NEUROLOGICAL BASELINE TESTING

Concussion management can include an athlete taking an exam before the season starts. This is called neurological baseline testing. A certified athletic trainer or medical professional usually oversees the exam. The test measures an athlete's motor, sensory, and cognitive functions. These include learning and memory skills, ability to pay attention and concentrate, and the time it takes to solve problems. The test also tests for any concussion symptoms. The results establish a baseline that can be compared to a similar exam during the season if an athlete is suspected of a concussion. This tool is also key in aiding a doctor or a trainer in evaluating a player for safe return to play.

The education depended both on the sport and gender. In football, preseason concussion education was given nearly 100 percent of the time. However, it occurred only 65 percent of the time with boys' ice hockey. It occurred just 57 percent of the time for boys' soccer. For girls' soccer the number dropped to 47 percent of the time.

The study also looked at sideline testing. These tests take place after a big hit. They look for signs of symptoms of cognitive and balance problems. But the study found that sideline testing was not consistently used during games and practices. Athletic trainers used this method about 75 percent of the time. In football and hockey it was used half the time. For boys' soccer it was used 30 percent of the time. And in girls' soccer it was only used 17 percent of the time.

IF HE ONLY KNEW THEN

Some athletes might suffer concussions without even knowing. Those who continue to play after a concussion might not have any problems at first. But eventually it catches up with them, experts say. Brian Lilja was a patient at Boston Children's Hospital's concussion clinic. He suffered two concussions while playing football as a high school freshman. Each time he kept playing. At the time, he didn't know he had concussions.

Then came his third concussion while he was playing lacrosse. This time he couldn't do anything. It took seven months before his symptoms lessened and he was able to resume a school schedule.

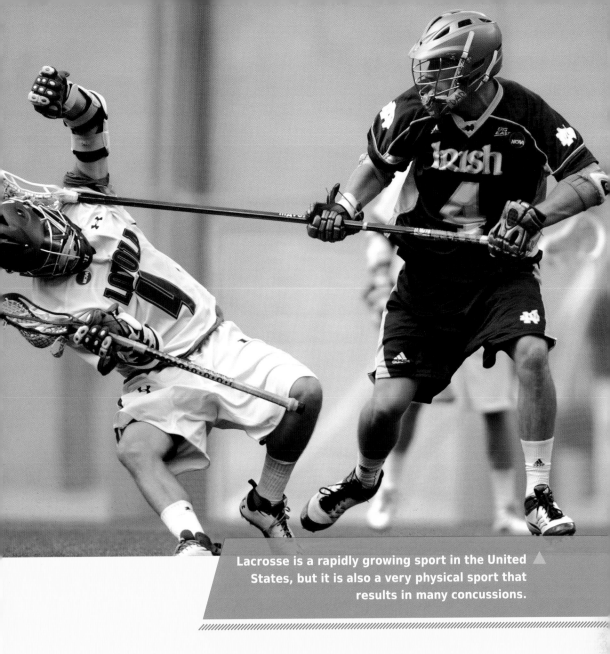

Lacrosse is a rapidly growing sport in the United States, but it is also a very physical sport that results in many concussions. ▲

"I read every story about concussions in the NFL and the NHL [National Hockey League], and I tell my friends and other athletes everything I've learned," Brian told the *New York Times*. "I wish I knew what I know now; I would have rested my brain after my first concussion."

CHAPTER 4

YOUNG BRAINS COLLIDING

How old should kids be when they play collision sports? For years that was mostly a question between parents and kids who wanted to play football. In recent years this question has come to the forefront on many levels.

Some people believe young athletes should not play collision sports. These people believe that a comparable hit to the head is more damaging in a young person than an older person. That is because young people's brains are not fully developed.

In New York, lawmakers proposed a ban on tackle football for children younger than 11. President Obama has even weighed in. He was asked

LATE BLOOMER TOM BRADY

Quarterback Tom Brady had played in five Super Bowls with the New England Patriots through 2013. He had won three rings. But he was not allowed to play football until he was 14. His parents didn't think he was physically developed enough until then. His father, Tom Brady Sr., said, "It's the same reason I wouldn't let him throw a curveball until that age. I told him, 'If I see you throw a curve, I will pull you right off this field,' and he knew I meant it. This head thing is frightening for little kids. There's the physical part of it and the mental part—it's becoming very clear there are very serious long-term ramifications."

if he would let a son play football. Obama doesn't have a son. If he had one, however, he said he would have to think twice about letting him play due to the concussion risk.

Not everyone agrees. Some youth league officials say that kids don't move or collide very fast. The lower speeds decrease the risk of concussions. One study compared the rate of concussions among different age levels. It found the rate for 8- to 10-year-olds to be nearly three times less than that for 11- and 12-year-olds.

John Butler is the executive director of Pop Warner Football. More than 250,000 children play in those leagues each year. Butler says kids are more likely to get concussions from other activities than youth football. Studies back up his claim. Approximately one-third of all concussions in children are from bicycling and skateboarding. In younger children, most head injuries are from falls or play during recess.

Parents are pretty much caught in the middle. They want to give their children the best chance to succeed now and later in life. So there are many disagreements. For example, USA Hockey banned body checking for boys below the age of 13. The goal was to keep kids safe and help them focus on fundamentals. However, some parents argued the rules would set their children back. The parents worried that kids who learned to check from an early age would get a competitive advantage. The same arguments exist in tackle football.

Dr. Robert Cantu is codirector of the Center for the Study of Traumatic Encephalopathy at Boston University School of Medicine. He is a leading expert in the study of sports-related concussions. Cantu believes that major steps should be taken to protect young brains. Cantu issued three warnings. 1. No one under the age of 14 should play a collision sport. 2. Heading the ball in soccer below age 14 should be banned. 3. Body checking in youth hockey should be banned until the age of 14.

Cantu says he is concerned not just with concussions but also with total brain trauma. Young athletes experience many blows to their brains. This is especially true for football players. These continuous blows are called subconcussive hits. Most of these hits do not cause a concussion. However, Cantu and others believe that concussions and subconcussive hits can contribute to Chronic Traumatic Encephalopathy (CTE). CTE is a degenerative disease caused by total brain trauma, according to the CDC. That means it gradually gets worse. CTE causes personality changes, memory loss, depression, and dementia. The symptoms usually don't show up until later in life.

Cantu says there are people who never had a recognized concussion but had CTE. He said the athletes who generate the most head trauma

tend to have higher amounts of CTE. So the football linemen who bash heads every play are most at risk.

CTE has been found in the brains of deceased football players. Previously researchers reported it was found only in the brains of deceased boxers. This disease was formerly called dementia pugilistica.

"We have millions of youngsters putting their heads into collision sports right now and we don't really know how safe this is for them," Cantu said.

However, other experts are not ready to accept that multiple hits or blows to the brain can cause CTE. They are waiting for more information to come out. CTE is a clinical diagnosis, and cannot be confirmed until a person dies and his brain is examined.

THE BOBBLEHEAD EFFECT

Experts do know that children are at a greater risk for concussions than adults. There are several reasons. Neck strength is very important to help protect against concussions. Strong neck muscles help the body to brace for a hit. This can lessen the force to the brain. But children don't have strong necks. And they have large heads. In a way they are like bobblehead dolls. The weaker the neck, the more the head will bob around on impact. It takes less of a jolt to impact the brain.

This is in part because children are always growing. And the growth is not always balanced. From ages five to eight a child's brain and head are disproportionately large. So children have a large and heavy brain and a weaker neck. This puts them more at risk for brain trauma when taking a hit. These conditions can last until around age 14. By then, a child's skull is about 90 percent the size of an adult's.

In addition, children's brain axons do not have a protective coating of myelin. Axons carry signals to other cells. The coating strengthens axons to help survive a concussive force.

Girls in general are more likely to suffer concussions than boys in the same sport. Girls have smaller heads but weaker necks than boys. Their necks are less developed. So they don't absorb the shock of impact as well as boys. This makes them more vulnerable to concussions. One study found that girls' soccer players suffered concussions 68 percent more often than boys' soccer players. The difference is even greater in basketball. When girls get hit in the head, their necks rotate faster than a boy's. This increases the force of acceleration of the brain. Experts say that girls are also more likely to get concussions because of hormonal differences.

STRENGTHEN THAT NECK

One study surveyed more than 6,700 high school soccer, basketball, and lacrosse players. It showed that the athletes with the weakest necks suffered the greatest number of concussions. The odds of getting a concussion fell by 5 percent for every one-pound increase in total neck strength. Neck strengthening exercises are easy. Use your own hands as a resistance tool. Put your hands on the back of your head. Then press them forward while your bend your neck backward.

CONCERNS WITH THE HEADER

Subconcussive hits are those blows that jolt the brain but aren't hard enough to cause a concussion. They do not cause immediate symptoms. Some researchers believe that repetitive subconcussive hits might contribute to CTE. Others point out that we are only just beginning to understand CTE. There could be a danger, they say. But they don't believe

there is enough information yet to force significant changes. Either way, people are paying attention.

Subconcussive hits are a concern for more than just football players. There can be subconcussive hits in any sport where there is head impact. In fact, heading a ball in soccer is a subconcussive hit. Studies are showing that repeatedly heading a soccer ball might increase the risk of brain injury. But the number of hits that could put a young athlete in danger is not quite clear. And most of these studies are of adult players who have played since childhood. One study showed that significant injuries occurred when a player headed a ball 1,000 to 1,500 times per year. Soccer balls can travel at speeds as high as 34 mph (54.7 km/h) during recreational games. They can travel more than twice that speed at the professional level.

More than 18 million people in the United States play soccer. And 78 percent of them are under the age of 18. "Brain injury due to heading in children, if we confirm that it occurs, may not show up on our radar because the impairment will not be immediate and can easily be attributed to other causes like ADHD or learning disabilities," said Dr. Michael Lipton of the Albert Einstein College of Medicine.

Lipton hopes excessive heading can be defined and guidelines can be established for safer play, like other sports have done.

PREVENTION, INVENTION, AND INTERVENTION

The evidence was growing. Photos of brains showing severe brain trauma and CTE in middle-aged former NFL players were piling up. The stories behind the photos were tragic. Many of the players had suffered for years from mental problems. Some of these players had committed suicide.

Lawsuits against the NFL were piling up, too. Researchers and widows of football players begged the NFL to listen. They pointed to the science that the former players' brain trauma was linked to blows the brain suffered playing the game. But the NFL denied there was a connection. Then, one day, the NFL listened.

▲ Oakland Athletics batter Aaron Cunningham left a 2009 game with a concussion after being beaned in the head by a pitch.

The real change to make all sports safer to play began on October 28,

2009. Congress called on experts to discuss the link between football and

permanent mental problems. The experts spoke for hours. Meanwhile, the NFL brought its own experts who denied the link. Panelists pleaded with the NFL to take concussions seriously and make football safer. They believed changes in the NFL would set the example for the millions of kids who play.

No words spoke louder than those of a father who had lost his son during a football game. Will Benson had been a high school quarterback. He collapsed and died during a game just two weeks after suffering a concussion. He died from second-impact syndrome. His brain had suffered another jolt before the first had healed.

"Don't let it happen again, please," said Dick Benson, Will's father.

A month after the hearing, NFL commissioner Roger Goodell changed course. He announced changes to NFL rules. The changes were meant to protect the health and safety of the players. He hoped they would also set an example "for players at all levels and in all sports."

The new rules said that any player with signs of concussion must be removed from a game or practice. The player would not be allowed to return the same day. The signs of concussion include a gap in memory, inability to remember plays, or amnesia. And the symptoms just had to be there once. The player would not be allowed to return that day even if the symptoms went away quickly. And players could only return once cleared by a medical professional. If any concussion signs remained, a player remained sidelined.

PREVENTION SUCCESS

The football team at Steamboat Springs High School in Colorado had 13 concussions during the 2011 season. In 2013, that number dropped to four. The drop was no coincidence. The team's booster club donated $28,000. That helped the program buy 67 new helmets and update 10 more. The team also bought facemasks, chin straps, and mouthpieces that were designed to reduce the risk of concussions. Before the season the team used baseline neurological testing. In addition, the team emphasized jaw and neck exercises. The players practiced proper tackling technique. On hitting days, the players also wore Guardian Caps. The caps go over helmets and are designed to reduce impact, according to the company that makes them.

Another major move was to bring in outside physicians to make these decisions. NFL teams already had team doctors. But team doctors work for the team. Sidelining a player could be a hard situation for team doctors. Outside physicians were not influenced by the team's needs. These doctors could make decisions based only on the well-being of the athlete.

It was a start. A big start. Since then, the NFL has become a leader in concussion awareness, research, education, and legislation. Rules on age-old practices have been changed. Helmet-to-helmet hits were outlawed. One high-profile rule makes it a 15-yard penalty whenever a player lowers his head and rams the crown of his helmet into an opponent. The rule is in effect if the hit takes place outside the pocket. This is the area of the field between the two offensive tackles. Some running backs were not happy about this rule change. They lower their helmets to protect themselves and the ball. But the rule stands. The NFL has become tougher. And all of this is causing a trickle-down effect.

During a 2011 protest, a young Canadian hockey ▲ fan urges hockey officials to make the sport safer and further penalize shots to the head.

CHANGING THE YOUTH GAME

Once the NFL acted, it didn't take long for youth organizations to follow. USA Football governs play in many youth leagues. In 2010, it toughened its rules against head hits. Players were no longer allowed to use their shoulders or forearms to contact an opponent above the shoulder. USA Hockey governs youth hockey. It has been a leader in concussion prevention. In 2011, USA Hockey outlawed body checking for boys under age 13. Girls cannot check at any age. A Canadian study surveyed two provinces. Body checking was allowed in Alberta but not in Quebec. The study found concussion rates in 11- and 12-year-olds were four times higher in Alberta than in Quebec.

Practices are also coming under the spotlight. Some youth leagues, high schools, and college conferences are limiting full-contact drills in practices. This is to limit the number of head hits and possible concussions. In 2012, Pop Warner responded to research that the hardest hits in youth football come in practice. The league limited contact among its 285,000 youth players to two-thirds of each practice. It also banned head-to-head contact during full-speed drills, head-on blocking, and tackling from more than three yards apart.

Pop Warner made its changes after a study of second-grade football players came out. Virginia Tech and Wake Forest University conducted the study. It found that the average player had more than 100 head impacts during the course of 5 games and 10 practices. Most of the hits were moderate. However, some were equal to a big hit in college football.

A 2013 report, though, is challenging the practice of limiting contact in practices. The study of youth football players found that kids are more likely to suffer concussions in games than in practices. It argued that limited contact is a mistake. The researchers said kids need to learn how to properly tackle. One researcher said the worst cases of concussions he sees are at the beginning of the football season. That is because many kids are new to the sport. They have not yet learned to tackle properly. To that reasoning, Dr. Robert Cantu says that kids 14 and under should play flag football. He says they should learn how to tackle by using dummies and pads. Also, as many experts warn, the concern is about all the extra hits in practice, not just the concussions.

G-FORCE, IMPACT SENSORS, AND HIT COUNTS

In the study of second graders, impact sensors were installed in their helmets. These sensors measured the gravitational force (g-force) on the hit to the body. The sensors sent information to a smart phone or laptop computer on the sidelines. An alert was then triggered when the player suffered a head impact strong enough to be concussive.

Hit counts are also recorded on sensors. Plus some sensors measure the area of the head receiving the impact. There might be no concussion. But multiple big hits in one area might alert a coach to check out a player's technique. Sensors are available for football, hockey, lacrosse, and snow sports such as snowboarding. Sensors are also made for mouth guards and chinstraps.

///////////////////////////

HIT COUNTS

Hit counts in all sports are gaining attention. Chris Nowinski is the cofounder of the Sports Legacy Institute. He said research might never be able to say how many hits it takes to cause brain trauma. However, high school football players might take an average of 1,000 hits a season. Some players absorb as many as 2,500 hits. In football, linemen and linebackers take more hits. They have body impact on nearly every play. Nowinski and experts from youth sports organizations are working on hit count guidelines for all sports, including soccer, ice hockey, and rugby.

///////////////////////////////

HELMETS

Helmets don't prevent concussions. They do protect the skull from direct blows, however. There have been many improvements to helmets over the years. Football helmets used to have foam padding on the inside. Now many helmets have shock-absorbing disks. They lessen the impact of hits.

There is no government standard rating system for helmets. However, there is a website that displays ratings for adult football helmets. Virginia Tech's National Impact Database expects to release ratings on youth helmets in the spring of 2015.

Most schools and youth programs use reconditioned football helmets. That means the helmets have been improved to fit newer standards. Experts advise that helmets should be reconditioned every one to three years. In addition, helmets should not be used for more than 10 years.

STILL HAVE FUN

Concussions are a serious issue in sports at all levels. However, experts note that people do not have to live in constant fear of concussions. They tell parents to relax. The awareness, education, and rule changes in sports are making a difference. As scientists press on, so do sports professionals. There is a lot to discover about sports and brain injuries. That's one thing everyone seems to agree upon.

The NFL changed its policy to remove players from games for any sign of a concussion. Other sports organizations soon followed. But the book *The Concussion Crisis* asserts that the change in policy didn't automatically change the way coaches manage players.

> No sooner had the 2010 college football season kicked off than fans were treated to this nationally televised spectacle: a head coach berating his team physician on the sideline for refusing to let a star player return to the same game in which he'd been knocked unconscious. As soon as Dr. Sam Haraldson diagnosed a concussion based on loss of consciousness as well as problems with balance and memory, Texas Christian University running back Ed Wesley should have been sidelined automatically per the new NCAA policy. But Haraldson found himself debating the return-to-play issue with TCU coach Gary Patterson in full view of ESPN's cameras.

> Source: Linda Carroll and David Rosner. The Concussion Crisis: Anatomy of a Silent Epidemic. New York: Simon & Schuster, 2011. Print. 262.

Changing Minds

You are a reporter watching this incident play out on the sidelines. Write a short blog post about what medical reasoning Dr. Haraldson was following in removing Ed Wesley from the game.

Many experts say that while athletes must be careful, they should remember that sports are supposed to be fun.

NFL commissioner Roger Goodell said, "We want answers, but we're not going to wait for all of those answers to make the changes that we think are important, and—not just in our game but in all of sports—[we want] to try to make the equipment safer and do what we can with the rules. Those are changes that we can control now until science catches up and can answer some of those questions."

DISCUSSION QUESTIONS

Take a Stand

Most schools and organizations are required, some by a state law, to provide concussion education to parents and athletes of contact sports. Pretend your school has not provided concussion education to any players. Write an e-mail to your school's coach, principal, or athletic director explaining the importance of concussion education for players and athletes.

Dig Deeper

In chapter two, high school freshman Mark Gould talks about his reasons for not playing football the season after his concussion. Mark loved football, and yet he said that the decision to not play again was easy for him to make. Explain the factors that influenced Mark's decision. If you were in Mark's position, what would your decision have been and why?

Tell the Tale

Most states have passed laws for concussion safety. Chapter three discusses how these laws will not work unless athletes and coaches work together to either self-report or take action when recognizing signs of concussions. Write a short essay about how our sports culture makes concussion safety laws difficult for some athletes and coaches to follow. How can coaches encourage athletes to self-report symptoms?

GLOSSARY

axons
The threadlike fibers in the brain that transmit information from neurons. Axons can be stretched and sheared during a concussion.

cognitive
Relating to conscious activity in one's brain.

degenerative
Something that gets progressively worse.

hit counts
A measure to reflect the number of times an athlete's brain has received a damaging impact during a given time period.

impact sensor
Placed inside a helmet, chin strap, or mouth guard, these sensors measure how strong a force is to the body and head during a collision and can immediately alert sideline personnel.

post-concussion syndrome
When symptoms last more than 10 days after a concussion. The prolonged symptoms can cause physical and cognitive difficulties, making it a struggle to return to normal activities, such as school.

subconcussive hits
Blows that jolt the brain but aren't enough to cause a concussion. They do not cause immediate symptoms, but researchers believe they lead to overall brain trauma and possibly CTE.

traumatic brain injury (TBI)
A bump, blow, or jolt to the head or a penetrating head injury that disrupts the normal function of the brain and can cause permanent disability or death.

FOR MORE INFORMATION

SELECTED BIBLIOGRAPHY

Cantu, Robert, and Mark Hyman. *Concussions and Our Kids: America's Leading Expert On How To Protect Young Athletes and Keep Sports Safe.* New York: Houghton Mifflin Harcourt, 2012. Print.

Carroll, Linda, and David Rosner. *The Concussion Crisis: Anatomy of a Silent Epidemic.* New York: Simon & Schuster, 2011. Print.

de Lench, Brooke. *Home Team Advantage: The Critical Role of Mothers in Youth Sports.* New York: HarperCollins, 2006. Print.

Marar, Mallika, and Natalie M. McIlvain, Sarah K. Fields, R. Dawn Comstock. "Epidemiology of Concussions Among United States High School Athletes in 20 Sports." *The American Journal of Sports Medicine.* The American Orthopaedic Society for Sports Medicine, 27 Jan. 2012. Web. 26 June 2013.

FURTHER READINGS

Fleischman, John. *Phineas Gage: A Gruesome but True Story about Brain Science.* New York: Houghton Mifflin Harcourt, 2004. Print.

Moore, Adam. *Broken Arrow Boy.* Kansas City, MO: Landmark Editions, 1990. Print.

Moser, Rosemarie Scolaro. *Ahead of The Game: The Parents' Guide to Youth Sports Concussion.* Lebanon, NH: Dartmouth College, 2012. Print.

Simon, Seymour. *The Brain: Our Nervous System.* New York: HarperCollins, 2006. Print.

WEB SITES

To learn more about concussions in sports, visit ABDO Publishing Company online at **www.abdopublishing.com**. Web sites about concussions in sports are featured on our Book Links page. These links are routinely monitored and updated to provide the most current information available.

PLACES TO VISIT

Newport Sports Museum
100 Newport Center Drive #100
Newport Beach, CA 92660
949-721-9333
www.newportsportsmuseum.org
This museum aims to promote healthy lifestyles through its memorabilia and partnerships with famous athletes. In addition, the museum has free programs meant to help instill confidence in children and teens.

US Olympic Training Center
1 Olympic Plaza
Colorado Springs, CO 80909
719-866-4618
www.teamusa.org
The Colorado Springs Olympic Training Center contains top-end training facilities for US Olympic hopefuls. Many athletes live and train here year-round. A 45-minute tour is available to the public.

INDEX

ABOUT THE AUTHOR

Maryann Hudson has won numerous national and regional awards as an investigative sports reporter for the *Los Angeles Times*. In addition, she has written a book about girls' golf. She is a graduate of the University of Southern California's School of Journalism. She currently is a freelance writer and lives with her family in Pasadena, California.